TESTIMONIALS

"Sparkle! *is like a magnet for positivity and engagement. Picture your workplace buzzing with energy, where everyone is aligned with the mission and motivated to contribute. This book shows you how to build a culture that attracts and retains top talent, making your organization a place where people love to work.*

"*In* Sparkle!, *stories become your most powerful tool. Imagine weaving narratives that touch hearts, inspire action, and create lasting memories. This book teaches you how to craft and share stories that amplify your impact and resonate deeply with your audience.*

"Sparkle! *is your guide to creating powerful connections. Envision a network where synergy thrives, bringing together diverse talents and resources to achieve common goals. This book shows how to build a collaborative ecosystem that multiplies your organization's effectiveness.*"

— Mary Robinson
Founder, Good Grief and Founder, Imagine
CNN Hero

"It is refreshing to see that Sparkle! *tackles some of the most important things we teach in business school to some of the most successful for-profits. How an organization approaches leadership, culture, and marketing for both the internal and external members is vital to its success. The* Sparkle! *that one brings to the nonprofit is contagious but doesn't have to be innate and can, in fact, be taught. I recommend that we all take the time to learn how we can ignite the* Sparkle! *in our organization."*

— Shane Smith, PhD
Director, Jim Moran Institute for Global
Entrepreneurship
Founder, The Nice Guy Entrepreneur

"With Sparkle!, *Merle Benny has distilled decades of her experience and observations with nonprofits into a powerful and accessible guidebook to help nonprofit organizations thrive and shine. This book will help many organizations and leaders in their path to optimal success."*

— Kalpana Bhandarkar
Principal, Spring Bhee Advisory

"Merle Benny's wisdom, enthusiasm, and practical approach to captivating hearts and minds makes Sparkle! *essential reading for every nonprofit leader, no matter the size or scale of their organization."*

— Frank Abdale
Abdale Consulting, LLC

"Having worked and taught alongside Merle for several years, I was happy to see this little book that reflects her smart, fun style. It is an informative and useful guide for nonprofit organizations, as well as consultants serving the nonprofit sector."

— Maria Badali
Arkle Consulting Group

"Merle Benny shines as a passionate changemaker in the nonprofit world. In Sparkle!, *she shares invaluable insights for achieving nonprofit excellence, offering a treasure trove of clear, compelling messaging that resonates and inspires. Especially valuable in these challenging times, this book equips you with the skills and mindset to become an impactful leader and a beacon of light in the sector."*

— Bruce Arbit, MPA, CFRE
President, Mission Impact Advisors

"In order to sustain success and impact, organizations must embed themselves in a collaborative ecosystem. Benny understands both the importance and messiness of this reality. Sparkle! is a great resource for leaders in public, private and nonprofit work who want to create long-term impact in their community."

— Matt Spence
Executive Director, Learning Independence for Tomorrow

GREETINGS!

I'm so glad you found this little book.

Did you ever notice everything looks better when you are in a good mood? Colors are brighter, people are friendlier, and opportunity seems to pop up in unexpected places.

I hope you journey through this book with that mindset.

This is a nonprofit leadership book for founders, directors, staff, board members, and consultants.

I wrote *Sparkle!* while thinking of happy, fulfilling workplaces where people like you are doing good work and feeling really good about it—the kind of place where growth and opportunity make greatness possible.

Life is a journey. And mine led me here.

In my long career, I've been a consultant, speaker, workshop leader, writer, meeting planner, and business owner. I have a lifelong commitment to nonprofits. I'm a mom, wife, and friend. I care deeply about the work that nonprofits do for our world.

Today, I work to put all I know, learned, and experienced into helping nonprofit leaders and rising leaders. I train aspiring nonprofit consultants so they, too, can lift organizations. (Learn more at Nonprofitconsultantsinstitute.com.)

Enough about me.

I wrote this book for you, putting all I know into five steps that will lead you to create a happier, healthier organization.

Imagine your life in a growing organization that can raise the money it needs to serve more people. That's my dream for you!

I want to know you. As you go through the book, share your insights, aha moments, and victories.

For a lively, engaging conversation that will elevate your nonprofit, it would be my pleasure to speak on your podcast or at your next event. Visit Nonprofitchampion.com/speaker.

Warmly,

Merle

SPARKLE!

Create a Brighter, Stronger Nonprofit

Communicate Better, Raise More Money, and Grow Faster (For Nonprofit Champions and Visionary Leaders)

MERLE BENNY

Sparkle!
Create a Brighter, Stronger Nonprofit: Communicate Better, Raise More Money, and Grow Faster
(For Nonprofit Champions and Visionary Leaders)

ISBN: 979-8-89079-153-5 (hardcover)
ISBN: 979-8-89079-154-2 (paperback)
ISBN: 979-8-89079-155-9 (ebook)

Legal and Earnings Disclaimer

Dedication

To Joe Landi, my partner in life and work. Your humor and creativity brought us this far and will see us through.

CONTENTS

FOREWORD

When I first met Merle, I was a bit shocked. I had just won a startup hackathon with my idea for an app to bring people together over lunch, and I was riding the high of all the praise coming my way. Someone recommended I connect with Merle, so we met for lunch. As we talked, her feedback stood in stark contrast to what I had been hearing from everyone else. People were telling me my idea was destined to be the next big thing, but Merle saw the gaps in my strategy.

Merle pointed out where my plan lacked structure and foresight, offering insights no one else had. Her frankness was refreshing, and it immediately struck me that she was someone I needed in my corner.

From that day forward, Merle became a trusted mentor. She has a huge heart, but what sets her apart is how she combines that love and passion with grit, experience, and tenacity. Whether she was working in Manhattan's fast-paced advertising industry or leading nonprofits to new heights, Merle always found a way to drive results.

I've watched her inspire and coach nonprofit champions to do the hard work of making the world a better place—and she does so with a rare blend of compassion and realism. Merle doesn't just dream big; she teaches others how to turn those dreams into actionable success.

The lessons in *Sparkle!* are the culmination of Merle's life and experience. As she helped me navigate the challenges of running a business, one piece of advice sticks out. I was at a crossroads, juggling a lot of interest from corporate clients that paid handsomely but didn't fulfill me as my nonprofit work did.

Merle told me, *"Do what makes you excited to get out of bed in the morning."* I followed that advice, keeping my focus on impactful organizations like United Way and the Bill & Melinda Gates Foundation, and it has paid off more than I could have imagined.

As I grew my business to nearly 2 million dollars in annual revenue without any outside investment, Merle remained my mentor and accountability partner. Her guidance kept me going on the long days and through tough decisions, and I've never looked back.

This book reflects that same powerful mix of love and grit that Merle embodies. In a world where attention is scarce, *Sparkle!* offers a clear path to cut through the noise and make your organization shine.

Merle's formula may seem simple, but it is profound in its ability to transform your thinking and your work. Sure, you could skip ahead and just read the formula, but you'd miss out on the wisdom that Merle weaves throughout these pages—wisdom gained from decades of experience helping people stand out, create change, and make the world a better place.

As you turn the pages of *Sparkle!*, prepare for a wake-up call. Merle's voice is frank and inspiring like a well-balanced meal served up with sizzling bacon, fresh fruit, and a Hyppo pop from St. Pete for dessert. She offers the motivation and tools you need to make your vision a reality. I'm honored to have been a small part of her journey, and I know that, like me, you'll come away from this book with new clarity, purpose, and excitement for what's ahead.

— Alex Abell
Founder and former CEO of Lunchpool (2021 exit)
IT Leader, Oak Ridge National Laboratory
(operating on behalf of the US Department of Energy)

WHY THIS BOOK IS RIGHT ON TIME

The world needs stronger nonprofits now!

Take a minute to dream. Dream of a world without war or hunger. A world without disease or fear.

That's not the world we are living in.

Recent years have brought a global pandemic and extreme weather and have escalated violence in many parts of the world. Close to home, we see murder, racism, and homelessness rates rising. These crises affect you in your local community, your region, the country, and the world.

I have just lived through the threat of two hurricanes in two weeks. These caused flooding, destroyed homes, and killed people. What a stark reminder that we need the services of nonprofits to get us through the tough times in life.

Thankfully, you are doing your part to make the world better. Nonprofit Champions like you dream of what's possible and work hard to bring those dreams to life.

This is a guidebook for leaders—including founders, directors, staff, board members, and consultants—to easily read, share, and use in organizations of all sizes. Whatever your mission is or how long you've been around, this is written, with love, for you.

This book explores how to create a fast-growth organization.

Because nonprofits like yours solve big problems. They make life better. They create communities and safe havens. Nonprofits do the good work.

Yet, chances are, you struggle to build an organization that delivers on those dreams.

Ideally, every nonprofit would have the resources, people, and support to deliver services and create a better community.

Most organizations, and probably yours, face big obstacles:

- There's never enough time.
- Fundraising gets harder and harder.
- Salaries are low; turnover is high.

Right now, it is more important than ever that non-profits, including yours, are well-funded, operating at peak efficiency, and positioned for sustainable growth.

WHY *SPARKLE!?*

This book is serious fun. It's an easy read with lots of quick ideas, insights, and tips. As I wrote it, I was dreaming of creating organizations that have something extra that sets them apart. That led me to *Sparkle!*

Here's how I will use the term and its variations so we're on the same page.

> **Sparkle**
> *Verb*
> **to shine brightly with a lot of small points of light***

This perfectly defines what I want for your organization: shining brightly for everyone to see.

Those small points of light (Sparks) are you and everyone in your organization. As you *Sparkle!*, you attract attention.

> **Spark**
> *Noun*
> **a feeling or quality that causes excitement***

---

* *Cambridge Dictionary*

Sparks are magical. They get noticed and make people feel good. Throughout the book, I share ideas and tips for creating sparks both inside and outside your organization.

Sparkler
Noun
a person who creates Sparks for a nonprofit organization**

You are about to discover how to be a Sparkler! Sparklers are rising leaders, consultants, board members, founders, and directors in nonprofit organizations. They add Sparks to create an organization with *Sparkle!*

Now that you know my definitions, you'll see them throughout the book.

** my definition

WHY I'M WRITING THIS FOR YOU

I'm going to share a secret with you. It is what I learned about nonprofit growth.

This is my discovery story. I share it so you can see how I came to understand what makes an organization soar.

As a marketing communications expert, I had a gift to give. I wanted to take my 30 years of experience and skills and put them to work for nonprofits.

After all, I had been responsible for launching million- and billion-dollar tech startups. I was ready to give my time to the organizations I loved.

I wasn't new to the sector; I had been actively engaged, personally and professionally, my whole life. But now, it was finally time to devote all my resources to nonprofits. I was ready.

The transition went smoothly. New projects for museums, social services, colleges, healthcare, and others resulted in logos, websites, annual reports, videos, fundraising campaigns, and events.

But it wasn't enough.

I could not give them what they needed. And I wanted to know why.

I realized some organizations were more successful than others despite our best efforts. So, I dug deeper.

I wanted to know why some nonprofits grow quickly while others inch along. I discovered:

- ✓ It wasn't about who had the worthiest cause
- ✓ Or which founder had deeper pockets and better connections
- ✓ Or how emotional the mission was (think: babies and puppies)

What I learned surprised me.

It also made me very happy.

You see, the solution isn't expensive or even time-consuming. The skills and practices can easily be learned and adapted, becoming part of your culture. And the big bonus is that it results in a happier, more sustainable organization!

As I said, this is a guidebook for leaders—including founders, directors, staff, board members, and consultants—to easily read, share, and use in organizations of all sizes. Whatever your mission is or how long you've been around, this is written, with love, for you.

This book explores how to create a fast-growing organization.

HOW TO USE THIS BOOK

Take a break.

You've earned it.

A few deep breaths, a good stretch, whatever you need to get into a feel-good mindset.

Now, get ready to discover a path to make your life easier, your work rewarding, and your possibilities endless.

What you'll find in this little book can be used immediately at your organization. Each small step you take along the way will help you communicate more clearly, inspire others, and, ultimately, make a greater impact in the world.

You are doing critical work. You don't want to waste a minute. That's why it is so important for you to use and share this with others right away. You'll be sharing this with your staff, volunteers, and board members. It's that important.

Get ready for the aha moments.

This isn't like any other (long, boring) book you've read.

- It's an easy-to-use guide loaded with takeaways and action items.
- It's based on years of study, practice, and observation and uses proven strategies to deliver measurable results.
- I love a good story, and I've included several to entertain, inform, inspire, and help you on your journey to give your nonprofit the *Sparkle!* it needs to grow faster and raise more money.

What I am offering you is a path forward through communication and connection. You'll take away from this book a powerful yet easy approach to building a better organization.

My intention is for you to quickly (because I respect your time) learn and share so you create a more inclusive, open, and welcoming organization that attracts resources (money!), talent, and buzz.

Are you ready?

You are about to create some excitement. You will make it happen by following the plan I have mapped out for you. I'm right here, cheering you on!

Now, I invite you to take a few precious minutes for yourself so you can discover what's inside. Get comfy, refill that drink, and turn the page.

P.S. Grab some sticky notes or turn on the mic and be ready to capture those aha moments.

THE WORLD NEEDS
YOUR ORGANIZATION

You have a big job to do.

Let's take a look at the big picture.

Nonprofit organizations exist to make the world better. At times of crisis, uncertainty, and rapid change, they become more important than ever. Whether you are serving your local community or solving world problems, your services are important.

The world needs strong, well-funded organizations positioned for growth.

It needs your organization.

Think of the hundreds of thousands of people impacted by the work of nonprofits.

Nonprofits take the lead on providing services:

- Caring for the sick
- Protecting the vulnerable
- Educating the young

- Inspiring the fearful
- Consoling the grieving
- Sheltering the homeless
- Feeding the hungry

Nonprofits are committed to fighting for:

- Equity
- Justice
- Inclusion
- Peace
- Access

Nonprofits are a voice for those unable to speak for themselves:

- Animals
- Babies and children
- Incarcerated
- Immigrants

But most nonprofits are struggling.

Whatever the size, mission, location, or age of your organization, it's probably hurting. Some of the issues have been around for a long time. But others have recently made it more difficult for you to get the job done.

Some of these may sound familiar:

- Budget cuts
- High staff turnover

- An inactive board
- Funder's demands
- Never enough time!

For most, there's never enough money, time, or talent. Yet the work is more important than ever.

And, sadly, you may be losing faith in your commitment to do the good work—to make a difference. You are too bogged down with diversions. It's disheartening.

There doesn't seem to be a way out or up.

There's not enough time or money. You've lost track of what matters, why you existed in the first place. There's too much bureaucracy and not enough innovation. You're stuck.

You know you need an engaged board, an energetic and smart staff, willing volunteers, and happy donors to be truly successful. How do you make that happen? You already have enough to do.

You need a clear path forward. You need it now.

This book takes you through a few simple steps. You can begin right now. If you're not the executive director or founder, that's okay. You can use this guide wherever you are in the organization: communications, development, client services, the board, etc.

It's designed to give you a fresh, practical path and a bright outlook for the future, which is just what you need.

What if your nonprofit had the momentum, clear vision, and excited determination to change the world?

What if you started right now?

DEBUNKING THE MYTHS ABOUT WORKING AT A NONPROFIT

Myth #1: It's impossible to keep long-term employees.

Turnover is high in nonprofits. Yet, some organizations can retain employees. Happy employees feel appreciated and tend to stick around. The secrets to successful retention are revealed throughout this book. (Hint: It's not about money.)

Myth #2: Everybody hates meetings.

Many nonprofit employees tell me they want more meetings. What they really hate are dull, boring meetings where they don't have a chance to participate. But you can add *Sparkle!* to your meetings. Keep reading to find out how.

Myth 3: I know storytelling is important, but I'm not good at it.

Stories are magical. They bring your work to life and create emotional connections that add value while leaving a lasting impression. Luckily for you, this book reveals an easy formula so you can learn to tell a great story. You'll also discover how to collect and share stories so your whole organization contributes to an active Story Culture.

Myth #4: I'm not the CEO, so I can't have an impact.

There is a lot of work to be done, and the CEO or executive director can't do it alone. You are valuable no matter what level of experience or how long you have been with the nonprofit. This book shows how you, and everyone in the organization, have a role to play as a spokesperson, storyteller, and connector.

Myth #5: Our work isn't interesting enough/emotional enough to attract donors.

Everyone has their own emotional reactions. It's not all about kittens and babies. I have cried for buildings! Your work may not appeal to everyone, and that's okay. But knowing how to reach the ones who will respond is key.

THE MOST IMPORTANT THINGS IN THIS BOOK

This is just for you, a Nonprofit Champion.

You don't have time to waste!

Think of this as your little book of secrets. But be prepared to share it. Everyone in your organization will want a copy once they hear your enthusiasm!

You are busy. You are doing important work. But you may need an energy boost. This is it! That Spark you have been needing. Your magic formula is packed in this little book.

It's an action plan.

You will walk through five steps, one building on the next, to transform your organization without disrupting the important work you are doing. Each step offers a fresh outlook and an easily implemented approach to building a fast-growth organization.

It's a story book (a guide for how to create a Story Culture).

You have a story to tell. Everyone in your organization has stories to share. You are about to discover a simple formula for telling great stories and how to make storytelling part of your culture. Plus, you will hear success stories.

It's a handbook.

This little book is designed to be a handy reference for you. A quick look will help you find what you need to take action or share an action step with someone else.

It's a game-changer.

Nonprofits have been known to get in ruts. Some practices are old and tired. Some no longer serve you or your organization. *Sparkle!* is a fresh approach to communicating, working, and connecting to build a better organization that raises more money and delivers on its promise.

What if your organization had the magic formula to continue to grow and raise more money?

Use this little book of secrets to make that happen.

Get ready to create *Sparkle!* now.

SNAPSHOT: A BETTER WAY TO MAKE NONPROFITS WORK

You don't need more work.

What you may need is a *better* way to work and to make your nonprofit work better.

A simple method that builds on what you already have. One that puts your mission front and center while it creates opportunities for partnerships and a growing donor base.

All that and a happier, healthier workplace for you!

Sparkle! **builds on what you already have.**

It inspires and prepares you to share the great work you are doing with the world. And it makes it possible for you to feel good while you're doing it.

These are the building blocks of an organization with *Sparkle!*

VISION

Step 1: You have places to go! Your journey begins with a clear vision. Discover the words to communicate that vision, and you will be ready to share them with the world. That's a magic start, or restart, of your organization.

VOICE

Step 2: If one person sharing your vision is good, imagine multiplying that by 10, 100, or 1,000! Imagine beautiful, heartfelt, diverse voices sharing the good news and the great need.

STORY

Step 3: Stories are magical! When storytelling becomes part of your culture, that magic means happier, engaged employees and plenty of great news to share with the community.

SYNERGY

Step 4: Weaving a network of connections from many sectors puts you at the center of possibilities. Like a living database, it builds dynamic networks. That means more opportunities for you and, ultimately, for those you serve.

SPARKLE!

Step 5: It's the magical difference that makes your organization communicate better, raise more money, and grow faster. Plus, you'll love going to work every day.

Start where you are.

You may be in a senior position as the founder of your nonprofit, the executive director, or the board chair. Or maybe you're a director of development, marketing, or HR. Or you may be aspiring to one of those positions. Whichever it is, it's the right place to begin looking ahead to a happy, growing organization ready to take on the world.

Bring Sparkle! In-House

When you see this symbol, it means this (and more) is covered in the Sparkle! Action Plan, a private workshop for your organization. Go to www.nonprofitchampion.com/actionplan to learn more.

Does your organization Sparkle!?

Take The Nonprofit Champion Growth Readiness Assessment and find out. Go to www.nonprofitchampion.com/doyousparkle now.

WHAT HAPPENED TO
THE DREAM?

All nonprofits start with a dream. The founder wants something in the world to change. Whether your organization was born last year or 100 years ago, it was created with enough hope and enthusiasm to propel it forward. Momentum builds as they share the dream—for a while.

It's harder to keep the momentum when the excitement dies down.

The same is true for you. You signed on because you believe in the dream and want to do your part.

Remember when you were eager and full of energy?

Then, something went wrong. Maybe now you feel left out or overworked. Maybe you feel unheard.

You may find it hard to maintain the traction you need for the good of the organization.

You are frustrated.

It's not your fault. And you are not alone.

Nearly one out of every five nonprofit employees voluntarily leave their jobs each year.

You want to work in a respectful environment that recognizes good work and hears your voice. You want that for yourself and for everyone else in the organization.

Imagine working every day with your heart full.

Imagine feeling inspired to share your thoughts and ideas with your coworkers.

Imagine them wanting to hear your story.

That's what you deserve. It's time to dream again.

MY HERO AND FIRST NONPROFIT CHAMPION

I love nonprofits. It all started in the Brownies.

My love for nonprofits started when I was seven. They have been at the center of my life ever since.

My mom signed me up to be a Brownie. (They were the youngest Girl Scouts back then.) I wore a brown uniform and a little beanie on my head.

As a clumsy left-hander, I failed at crafts. I couldn't carry a tune, so they shushed me when it came time to sing the "Brownie Smile Song." I certainly didn't win the prize for selling the most cookies; it didn't help that I had an older sister who got to every house before me.

But I fell in love with Juliette Gordon Low.

Juliette was the founder of Girl Scouts. When I heard her story, she became my hero. Imagine a seven-year-old girl hearing about a spunky woman who traveled to England, heard about the Boy Scouts, came back, and started a movement of her own—just for girls like me.

I discovered there were other Brownies in my town, in other parts of New Jersey, and all over the United States. I was part of something big, thanks to Juliette.

Over the course of my childhood and teen years, I was a Brownie, a Junior, a Cadette, and a Senior Girl Scout. I went on to be a Girl Scout Leader and, like Juliette, traveled to England. (Maybe I was braver than her; I took eight 15-year-old girls with me!)

On my journey with the organization, I came to see the value of nonprofits. I learned how they enrich my life and how I can enrich others' lives through them.

The founder of Girl Scouts remained my hero. Over time, I came to realize that I didn't want to be Juliette Low; I wanted to create more Juliette Lows.

My career took lots of turns, and my nonprofit employment didn't go so well (more on that later). But I believe in nonprofits. I love the people who work so hard to make them possible.

Thank you. You are my hero.

You inspire me to continue to support, champion, and celebrate great nonprofit organizations and the people who build them.

You, like Juliette Low, are a Nonprofit Champion.

MY STORY IN FOUR ACTS

Life is a journey. I see it like a snowball, rolling along, picking up more snow as it goes until it becomes big and strong enough to support other snowballs.

My greatest joy is in supporting rising nonprofit leaders. That's why I'm writing to you—and for you.

I'd like to share my story with you. I'm going to pack a long career into a short bio. It will help you see how my experiences led to the insights and discoveries I share with you in this book.

Act 1

I hear young nonprofit employees say how frustrated they are.

They want to do good work, but something gets in the way: low pay, an unfriendly work environment, lack of direction.

I was one of those workers.

After graduating from Rutgers University, I was ready to take on the world. My active campus leadership resulted in my being selected as the Valedictorian of my class. It was only the beginning.

I was eager and idealistic.

I got my first professional job at an inner-city community action organization. It was the 70s; activism was hot. I was assigned to work with teenagers. However, at 21 years old, I didn't feel qualified, so I struggled. Throw in sexual harassment from the boss, and it was a disaster.

Next stop, a Girl Scout council. Have I told you I love Juliette Low, the founder of Girl Scouts? This job did its best to end that love affair. I was shuffled off to a remote office, again with little direction, and told to keep the volunteers happy. I hope they were happier than I was.

That ended my nonprofit employee dream.

Act 2

I decided to go corporate.

By this time, I was a single mom; money was more important than ever. I landed a great job. The training was excellent. My work as a meeting planner was challenging, and I was surrounded by supportive coworkers.

I was on the corporate fast track. Soon, I was marketing and managing a national seminar program. I was hooked.

However, my desire to contribute to the important work of nonprofits stayed strong.

That meant lots of volunteering. I served on a community center board, spent many nights with homeless families, and co-chaired a capital campaign for a museum. When my daughter, Joy, was twelve, I became her Girl Scout Leader.

Meanwhile, I decided it was time for a greater work challenge. I was fortunate to land a job in the big city as the president of a Wall Street computer training company. I honed my marketing skills, tripling the offerings and the revenue in the first two years. Sadly, the corporate parent company decided they didn't want to be in the training business, and we closed it up.

My marketing success landed me a great opportunity at an advertising agency with major international tech clients. In addition to sharpening my marketing and writing skills, I met my future husband.

Act 3

I started my own marketing communications agency, servicing the rapidly growing tech sector. The work was exciting and gave me the opportunity to partner with my new husband, Joe. (Side note: We got married the same week Joy went off to college.)

Clients included Fortune 500 companies and the crazy geniuses rapidly becoming millionaires and billionaires, leading the way in the dot-com era. Working firsthand with these successful entrepreneurs taught me a lot about drive, communication, and connection.

As if life wasn't busy enough, we adopted two children—John was ten and Sarah, seven—when they joined our family. I was still volunteering as the board chair for a housing organization and an active leader in community and professional organizations.

Finally!

I worked my way back to where I always felt I belonged: helping nonprofit organizations form, grow, and thrive. All the experiences I had on my long journey informed my work to support and champion nonprofit organizations.

I've worked side by side with great nonprofit founders, executive directors, and CEOs.

I have also had the opportunity to mentor rising leaders in organizations—from newly formed local organizations to large, 100-year-old national and international nonprofits.

You see, along the way, I realized I didn't want to be Juliette Gordon Low; I wanted to create Juliettes. I wanted to help founders, leaders, and rising leaders make their mark and create great organizations that make our world a better place for everyone.

Quick Facts

Places I have lived: Cincinnati, Ohio; South Jersey; North Jersey; St. Petersburg, Florida

Favorite travels: Road trips in Europe, Canada, East and West Coasts USA

What I do when I'm not working: Read, walk, cook, and entertain (Did I mention I love working?)

What I've yet to do: Go to Scandinavia, give a TED talk, speak French fluently

How I start my day: Up by 5:00, do the *New York Times* puzzles, read the obituaries (great short bios), have an espresso, walk Fiona (our one-eyed Shorkie), go to the gym

My lifelong commitment to the work of nonprofits, like your organization, inspired me to write this book for you. I want every nonprofit organization to be a great place to work. I want you to do meaningful work. And while you are doing it, I want you to be happy, appreciated, and rewarded.

You are about to embark on a five-step journey. I promise you it will be insightful and inspiring. You will feel good about investing your time in reading this little book. You are about to begin on the path to *Sparkle!*

This book is written to make your journey the one that fulfills your dreams.

I'd love to hear from you along the way. Share your journey with me at merle@nonprofitchampion.com.

STEP 1: VISION

Your Journey to *Sparkle!* Begins

Start here. Be ready to discover a new way to see a future for yourself and your nonprofit organization.

I'll walk you through the five steps of your journey so you can discover how to become an organization that communicates better, raises more money, and grows faster. Along the way, you'll discover resources, action sheets to get you started, and case studies.

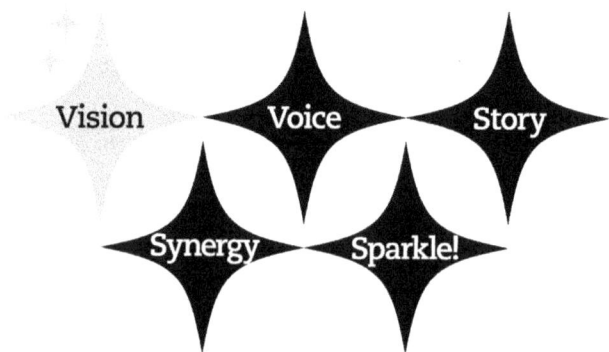

You will start with a vision. I'll show you why and how to use vision to attract the resources you need.

You'll discover how to find your vision and use it both inside your nonprofit and outside your organization.

Your vision is a game changer.

Let's take the first step.

Nonprofits: From Dream to Reality

Once upon a time, Juliette Gordon Low had a *dream* that girls would have the same opportunities boys had.

She imagined girls camping and hiking. Her *vision* was for girls to have outdoor adventures.

Juliette modeled the Girl Scouts of the USA on the Boy Scouts but created it uniquely for girls. The mission was to create Girl Scout troops all over the United States for girls from 10 to 17 years old.

Today, there are over two million Girl Scouts.

Dreams Do Come True

Nonprofit organizations like yours make the world a better place.

Nonprofits touch everyone. The work you are doing has an impact on others. And, chances are, you have enjoyed the results of another nonprofit organization's work.

Nonprofits are a spark that drives opportunity, generosity, and goodness.

For many, a nonprofit is the answer to a dream; they are often life-changing.

It All Starts with a Founder

Nonprofit organizations like yours usually start with one brave person.

Creating an organization requires a special drive, determination, and faith. First, you must recognize the need. Then, you must have the guts to take on a challenge. The motivation is not money, prestige, or power. It is about following a dream that will ultimately benefit others.

Nonprofit founders are dreamers.

You may have a founder who you know and admire, or you may be a founder yourself. As you may know, it takes big dreams to start a nonprofit organization.

It also takes hard work. But it is those dreams that inspire the founder to build something special.

Founders are young, old, rich, poor, novices, experts, and everything in between. There are no specific requirements. But it takes an incredibly special person to be a nonprofit founder.

Some are well-known. In 1938, President Franklin D. Roosevelt founded the March of Dimes. His paralysis inspired him to find a cure for polio. The organization fulfilled its dream of ending childhood polio and then went on to address other baby health and mortality issues.

Other founders use determination and hard work to make up for a lack of influence or power.

Agnes and Edgar Land wanted to preserve hand-crafted tools and the objects made from those tools. They turned their collection into the Museum of Early Trades & Crafts. The museum continues to provide the showcase, preservation, and education that inspired them to create it from little more than a dream.

Mary Robinson's dad died when she was a teenager. Inspired by her unresolved grief, she founded Good Grief, an organization for children who have lost a parent. She went on to found Imagine, A Center for Coping and Loss. Mary dreams of a world where no child grieves alone.

Dreaming of a Better World

Working with Agnes, Mary, and other dreamers, I have seen how a founder ignites action and change. Working with large national and international organizations, I have seen how a founder's influence can last decades, even a century.

As a founder, you need strong determination, creativity, and commitment.

And you need people.

People who believe in your dream.

Dreams are the start of an organization. They are the spark that makes everything else possible. Long before there is a vision, mission, or strategic plan, there is a dream that something will be different, better, easier.

Unfortunately, organizations may lose that spark. The dreams may be replaced by day-to-day concerns and deadlines.

A nonprofit organization is an entity created and operated for charitable or socially beneficial purposes rather than to make a profit.

In the United States, many of our largest nonprofits are over 100 years old.

Since the 1980s, the number of nonprofits has multiplied all over the world. There are now over 10 million organizations worldwide; 1.8 million of them are in the United States.

One hundred thousand nonprofit organizations are founded each year in the United States. Their scope may be global, or they may serve a small community, or somewhere in between.

Nonprofit organizations, most often classified as 501(c)(3) in the USA, may be formed to address a specific need in these or other categories: religion, human services, health, education, arts, environment, and animals.

A Vision of a Better Future

Nonprofits start with dreams. Your founder had a dream. Without it, they would not have been inspired to create an organization.

Going from dream to vision brought your founder closer to starting a nonprofit.

Your founder was a visionary.

Dreams are often hazy. Like the dreams we have in our sleep, they may fade quickly. It is turning that dream into a vision that gives it form. A vision paints a picture and is easily explained in words.

Juliette Low went from dreaming about opportunities for girls to something clearer and more specific: outdoor adventures. It's possible to imagine her, over 100 years ago, talking about girls hiking and camping. You can almost smell the campfire. She shared a vision.

Building a Strong Organization

Your dreams keep you hopeful; they inspire you to keep going even when the work is challenging.

But it takes more than a dream to build a sustainable, growth-oriented organization.

What does it take?

To grow a sustainable organization, these are some considerations:

1. Be guided by your vision.
2. Deliver on your mission.
3. Create a sharing and learning environment.
4. Value teamwork and internal communication.
5. Find and keep good employees at all levels.
6. Recruit, honor, and engage board members and other volunteers.
7. Build an ever-growing network of donors and partners.

Each of these sustainability points will be covered throughout this book.

Vision is a starting point. Without it, there is no direction.

Vision is being able to see what might be possible. It is broad enough to be open to possibilities but specific enough to create clear objectives.

Vision takes you from a dream to a mission. It has a unique and valuable place in your organization:

Vision is both a driving force and a magnetic attraction.

Vision is a driving force inside your organization, and you need to be inspired every day.

Vision is a magnetic attraction, allowing you to share your vision with others who come to care about your vision, share it, and take action to make it grow and prosper.

In the pages ahead, you will discover the magic of your vision. Be ready for those aha moments that will inspire you and prepare you to grow your organization.

Vision Statements

Organizations like yours may create vision statements. These are great starting points for talking about your vision. There are many examples of good ones. They tend to be short and get right to the point.

Read these examples of vision statements from global organizations and think about what they mean to you. Can you relate to them? Do they make the organization's vision for the world clear?

> Alzheimer's Association: *A world without Alzheimer's disease*
>
> Habitat for Humanity: *A world where everyone has a decent place to live*
>
> CARE International: *A world of hope, tolerance and social justice, where poverty has been overcome and all people live in dignity and security.*

Take another look. Notice that they don't talk about the work they are doing toward that vision. These visions could be shared by several organizations, each taking a different path to achieve the vision. Those separate paths are missions.

Before we get to your mission, let's explore how vision works so well as an internal driving force *and* external magnetic attraction.

Bring Sparkle! In-House

This (and more) is covered in the Sparkle! Action Plan, a private workshop for your organization. Go to www.nonprofitchampion.com/actionplan to learn more.

Does your organization Sparkle!?

Take The Nonprofit Champion Growth Readiness Assessment and find out. Go to www.nonprofitchampion.com/doyousparkle now.

Vision – Internal Sparks *and* External Sparks

Now, let's take a closer look at how vision works inside your organization. Then, I'll share some benefits you may experience outside of your organization as you interact with individuals, funders, and the public.

Internal Sparks: Discover How Vision Makes Magic Inside Your Organization

Imagine this:

You are in a hurry. You have places to go.

You get in your car, turn on the engine, and kick it in gear. But wait!

You can't see a thing. The windows are fogged up. The wipers do nothing to help. The problem isn't on the outside; it is inside your car.

Of course, you are not ready to move forward. You're stuck until you have a clear vision.

A Clear View for a Better World

Your nonprofit organization may be like that foggy car. It functions, but its path forward isn't clear. Like the car, the problem is internal.

That's frustrating.

Nonprofit organizations need a clear path forward so they can continually grow, raise more money, and serve more people.

A shared vision gives you that path. It is your driving force.

Chances are your organization started with a clear vision. That is how the founder was able to get support, funding, volunteers, and board members (more on attraction to come).

The need to share a common vision may be forgotten as the organization grows. But it remains a key factor in growth and sustainability.

Without a clear vision, you may miss out on:

1. **Working with a shared direction:** Your vision guides choices and decisions, aligning your work and keeping you focused on your goals.
2. **Engaging staff, board members, and other volunteers**: When everyone working for and with your organization has a clear message to share about the vision, they are more fully engaged— and may even become great spokespersons and fundraisers.
3. **Building an ever-growing network of donors and partners**: A vision-driven organization has the potential to attract a continually growing

circle of influence. Those who share your vision become donors, advocates, and partners (much more on this to come in Step 4: Creating Synergy).

Vision is a force that propels you forward.

A clear and compelling vision results in a clear and compelling message.

That's powerful!

Bring Sparkle! In-House

This (and more) is covered in the Sparkle! Action Plan, a private workshop for your organization. Go to www.nonprofitchampion.com/actionplan to learn more.

Does your organization Sparkle!?

Take The Nonprofit Champion Growth Readiness Assessment and find out. Go to www.nonprofitchampion.com/doyousparkle now.

External Sparks: Discover How Vision Makes Magic Outside Your Organization

Vision is a magnetic attraction.

Vision propels your organization forward, but that's not all it does. Your vision also attracts others to care, give, and get involved.

Vision is your secret tool for growth and opportunity. And, yes, it is a fundraiser.

As you will discover throughout this book, communication is key to nonprofit organizational growth. The words you speak, share, and repeat have an impact. Here's the secret: All those powerful communications start with a vision.

Vision is Your Sparkle!

A fast-growth organization needs:

1. A compelling message that grabs attention and piques interest
2. A consistent presence in places, online or off, that it can be seen and heard
3. Many voices and diverse voices to appeal to a broader audience

It all starts with getting your message right. That's where vision comes in. It is the sweet spot—right between your dreams and your mission.

Vision is broad enough to appeal to many different people. It is also specific enough to start a conversation, find common ground, and make a connection.

Remember those examples:

> *A world without Alzheimer's disease*
>
> *A world where everyone has a decent place to live*
>
> *A world of hope, tolerance, and social justice, where poverty has been overcome, and all people live in dignity and security.*

They are hard to argue with. More importantly, they are easy to talk about, become emotional about, and share.

As you journey through this book, you will see that every aspect of your success counts on connecting, sharing, and building an ever-growing network. Vision is the place to start.

Dream   →   # Vision   →   Mission

Your ideal.   Your objective.   Your plan.

Why Does Vision Come Before Mission?

You may have heard you should share your mission first. After all, your mission is the important work you do. Fight the temptation! It's vital, but it is not your opening statement.

Simon Sinek has one of the most viewed TED talks of all time. In his talk, *How Great Leaders Inspire Action*, he delivers the message that successful people and organizations communicate differently. Their compelling messages start with *why* they do what they do rather than what they do or how they do it.

Your Vision is your *why*.

Your mission is what you do and how you do it.

According to Sinek, "People don't buy what you do; they buy why you do it." It is not facts and figures that drive decisions. Decision-making is emotional. That is why you connect with people who believe what you believe. These believers become your driven employees, dedicated volunteers, and major donors.

Sinek uses Dr. Martin Luther King's famous "I Have a Dream" speech, delivered in 1963 to 250,000 people on the steps of the Lincoln Memorial in Washington DC, as an example of sharing a Vision. That huge crowd gathered because they believed what he believed. They shared his dream.

To further drive the point home, Sinek points out that MLK said, "I have a dream," not, "I have a plan."

Your Vision tells why you do what you do. Start there, and your message will resonate.

Seeking a broader audience and connecting with others who share your vision—yet have different missions—opens opportunities.

To engage, inspire, and ignite your audience (of one or 1,000), start with your vision for a better world, the reason your organization exists.

We will take a deep dive into speaking about your vision in Step 2: Giving Voice to Vision.

Bring Sparkle! In-House

This (and more) is covered in the Sparkle! Action Plan, a private workshop for your organization. Go to www.nonprofitchampion.com/actionplan to learn more.

Does your organization Sparkle!?

Take The Nonprofit Champion Growth Readiness Assessment and find out. Go to www.nonprofitchampion.com/doyousparkle now.

Action Sheet – Vision

Your Dreams

Daring to dream creates magic. Envision allowing yourself space to dream about what could be. As we explore what Sparkle! adds to your organization, the space to dream and share dreams will be central to the concept.

Reflect on the dreams of your founder.

> What motivated the founder to start your organization?

> Does your organization still share those dreams?

> If your founder is still active in the organization, talk to them about their dreams.

Reflect on your dreams.

> Think about the dreams you have for your organization.

> Do you have dreams that might inspire you to be a founder?

> Does your organization take time to dream?

STEP 2: VOICE

Your Vision, Your Voice, Your Sparkle!

As you've just read, sharing your vision is your first key growth step.

Remember, vision is the sweet spot between your dream and mission. It has a unique and valuable place in your organization.

A clear and compelling vision results in a clear and compelling message.

Using your voice to share that message allows others to see what might be possible and invites them to be part of it.

Read this section to discover how you and everyone in your organization can turn this simple tool into a powerful driver.

Voice is the next step on your path to a happier, healthier organization.

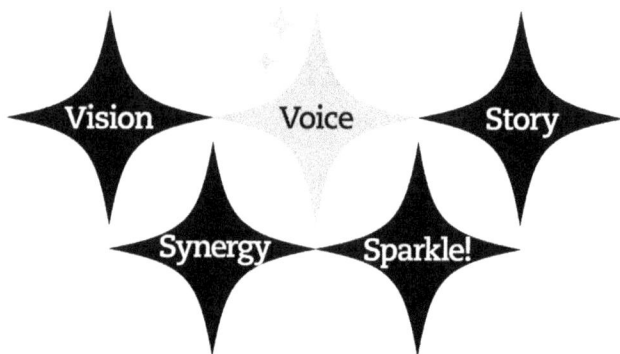

Sharing your organization's vision is a key step in building a sparkling, growing, dynamic nonprofit. Encouraging others to use their voices multiplies the impact.

That's powerful.

Using Your Voice

If you are the founder, director, manager, development officer, or rising leader, you may use your voice to grow your organization.

When you are talking to one person or a crowd, posting on Facebook, sending an email, or writing a grant application, you are using your voice to share information that inspires others to care and act.

Take a few minutes to think about how important communication is to the success of your organization.

It's pretty important! Right?

Your voice matters. You may use your unique voice to:

1. Give praise, explain a problem, and tell a story
2. Share information, inform the public, and request a donation
3. Offer services, assist clients, and explain procedures

Good communication is needed internally to get the job done and externally to continue to grow.

Want to add Sparkle! to your nonprofit consulting practice?

If you have experience working with nonprofit organizations and want to help your clients clarify their vision and use the Sparkle! Action Plan to raise more money and grow faster, take the first step to become a Certified Sparkle! Guide. Apply today at www.nonprofitchampion.com/certification.

Opening the Conversation

The lady behind you in the grocery line won't ask your age. The guy at the bar won't ask where you live. But it seems that anyone and everyone might ask this question:

"What do you do?"

Your answer to this question has the potential to be the start of a great conversation. It may lead to a new volunteer, advocate, or board member. Or it may result in a donation. The possibilities are endless—especially when you are prepared to answer it.

When I ask that four-word question, I often get a long answer that includes a job title, daily tasks, technical jargon, and other wordy descriptions. What I really want to hear is what gets you out of bed in the morning, what you care about, and why your work is important to you.

Start with Vision

Vision is how you kick it off. Use your voice to share the vision of your organization.

Speaking about your vision opens a path to connection.

When you speak about your vision, you may:

✓ Easily make a connection

✓ Generate interest, concern, or emotion
✓ Inspire questions and follow-up

Quick reminder: Start with your vision—not your mission. When someone asks about your work, they don't want the details. It's not about the work you do; it is about why you do it. vision is a great opening to what could become a memorable exchange.

More of What You Want

Your voice is a tool you can use to get more of what you want for your organization.

As a nonprofit leader, you know what you need for success.

Chances are, your organization needs:

✓ More money
✓ Dedicated employees
✓ Active board members
✓ Engaged volunteers
✓ Satisfied clients
✓ Access to opportunities

Your voice may inspire all of those. But it's not only *your* voice! Imagine many voices sharing the same vision. The power and possibilities are multiplied.

More Voices, More Impact

Sharing the good work of your organization is a powerful yet easy way to inspire others to care.

When you speak about vision, you are a source of inspiration. You are making connections. You are creating possibilities. Imagine multiplying that impact many times over.

That's what happens when everyone in your organization has a voice.

You, together with the many diverse voices from your organization, have the power to inspire others to care, to act, and to give.

Speaking about your organization isn't your job? Your job description may not say anything about marketing, communications, or fundraising. Those are specialized roles, and it is important to follow their guidelines and make referrals to them.

But life gives you lots of opportunities to get the ball rolling in their direction.

Once upon a time…

Jim retired, giving him free time to pursue his passions. That meant he was playing more golf than ever! He was also quite active in his church. That's what led him to become a board member of an organization that provides support and services for single moms.

Jim has a big heart and cares deeply about the work of the organization; his mom raised him alone after his dad's sudden death.

Unfortunately…

Jim wanted to share the good news of the organization with his friends. He knew they could be helpful as volunteers and donors. But every time he tried to talk about it, he got uncomfortable and was at a loss for words.

Thankfully…

The organization offered new training for staff, volunteers, and board members to help them speak about the good work of the organization and why it is so important right now. At the training, Jim had the opportunity to reflect on why it mattered to him and practiced speaking about his feelings with others.

Happily, ever after…

As a result, Jim was able to clearly talk about the vision of the organization. He used his voice to inspire others at church and on the golf course. He quickly discovered he was not alone; some of his buddies had personal stories to share. And many were happy to follow his lead and donate.

Creating Magic

You deserve some magic. Your nonprofit is making a difference in the world.

Continually expanding and creating opportunities requires great communication.

You can't do it alone.

The more voices you have comfortably speaking about your vision, the more attention you get, the more money you raise, and the more you deliver on your mission.

That's magic!

Everyone in your organization has a voice and, if encouraged and motivated, may use that voice to share the vision. Vision is the perfect opening to so many of the vital communications you, as a growing nonprofit, may have.

More Voices, More Opportunities

Your organization needs many voices.

Like a chorus, a nonprofit may be a great mix of voices working together. Each individual voice is special. The diversity of voices adds depth and reaches a broader audience.

You may find it hard to attract young volunteers, a racially diverse board, or some other demographic that may add value to your work. When everyone within the organization feels empowered to speak and share the vision, you reach a broader range of ages, life experiences, and talents.

As your organization grows, more people are impacted by your work. Your successful organization may:

1. Serve more people
2. Hire more staff
3. Build a larger board of directors
4. Attract more volunteers
5. Solicit more donors
6. Partner with other organizations
7. Work with government agencies
8. Benefit from corporate sponsorships

Using your unique voice to share your vision will help you attract more of what you need.

Great organizations, those that raise more money and grow faster, are made up of many voices. Each knows and understands the organization's vision and is *willing, able, and motivated* to speak about that vision for a better world.

A fully engaged employee or board member is willing, able, and motivated to use their voice to share the vision of your organization.

Voice – Internal Sparks and External Sparks

Now, let's take a closer look at how your voice works its magic inside your organization. Then, I'll share some of the benefits you may experience outside of your organization as you interact with individuals, funders, and the public.

Internal Sparks: How Voices Create a Better Workplace

A healthy nonprofit is a great place to work. What could be better than doing important, meaningful work in a supportive environment?

One strong indicator of a healthy, happy workplace is good communication. Unhappy employees often tell me they don't get enough information and they don't have a chance to share their ideas.

If you have ever worked in an organization where you didn't get information, weren't invited to share your thoughts, or felt left out, you know it hurts.

Not only that, but you may also not be able to do your best work.

Your organization has big challenges and big problems to solve. Poor communication makes them more difficult, plus it means less productivity and higher turnover.

Great communication starts inside your organization. An unhappy workplace is not the best groundwork for successful growth. A fertile landscape includes happy, motivated employees, volunteers, and board members. In turn, this creates happy donors.

What can you do about it?

Start where you are in the organization. You don't have to be the executive director or board chair. Look around.

- ✓ Do you have the information you need?
- ✓ Do you share ideas with your coworkers?
- ✓ Are the meetings you hold and attend productive?
- ✓ Do they allow time for feedback and sharing?

There may be some small changes you can make today that will feel good to you and to others. Communication is powerful.

Here are some ideas for creating a healthy workplace where everyone is *willing, able, and motivated* to use their voice.

1. **Become an active listener:** Start where you are with your friends, family, and coworkers. Ask questions and be ready to really listen to responses. Encourage others in your organization to share their ideas and be open to different views.

2. **Take time for personal reflection:** Think about the vision for the organization and ask yourself these three questions:

Why me? Reflect on your life and experiences and how they impact the work of your organization. Chances are you have a story to share.

Why us? Think about your organization and its work toward the vision for a better world. Your nonprofit has unique characteristics, benefits, and successes.

Why now? Consider this moment in time. Create a feeling of urgency by reflecting on why the work matters right now.

You may want to use this exercise with a group in your organization.

Marshall Ganz, a key thinker and educator at the Harvard Kennedy School - Harvard University, uses a storytelling approach to community organizing. The exercise above is adapted from the one he used to prepare volunteers for the first Obama presidential campaign. Like a political campaign, your organization relies on committed, informed workers.

3. **Pay attention to the small victories:** Good things happen in your organization every day. They are often overlooked or forgotten. Take a minute to write them down or share them. These Minor Miracles (more to come in the Story step of this book) keep you motivated.

When your organization creates the space to share Minor Miracles, you honor each person's contribution to the vision. They are also great material for grant applications, social media, and other public sharing.

You can be a catalyst for better communication inside your organization by using your voice and encouraging others to use theirs. Create that chorus of diverse voices internally, and you will create momentum to move your vision forward.

Bring Sparkle! In-House

This (and more) is covered in the Sparkle! Action Plan, a private workshop for your organization. Go to www.nonprofitchampion.com/action-plan to learn more.

Does your organization Sparkle!?

Take The Nonprofit Champion Growth Readiness Assessment and find out. Go to www.nonprofitchampion.com/doyousparkle now.

External Sparks: Many Voices Help Your Organization Grow

You may begin to see how speaking about what you care about—using your voice to speak about your vision—is a very powerful tool for you and your organization.

In his popular TED talk, *How Great Leaders Inspire Action*, Simon Sinek suggests you always start with why. Instead of talking about the features of a product, he suggests talking about the benefit to the user.

For you and your organization, your *why* is the change you are making for a better world; it is your *vision*.

Speaking to Inspire

Rather than selling more products, you, as a non-profit organization, are inspiring action, benefiting more people, and having a greater impact.

Giving everyone in your organization a voice to share your vision is your secret to success. That's Sparkle!

Think of all the opportunities you and your organization may have to share your vision. Stories are a great way to share and connect. We will take a deep dive into storytelling in the next section of the book.

One Clear, Compelling Message

Vision gives you and everyone in your organization one clear message. Your vision is your connection to the world around you.

> I remember sitting at Mary Robinson's kitchen table as she shared her vision for a new organization with me. Mary's vision became Imagine, a Center for Coping with Loss. Ten years later, on national television, I watched Mary, standing next to Anderson Cooper, as she repeated the same vision—that no child should grieve alone—as she was honored as a 2019 CNN Hero.

Corporations spend millions to create a message and send it out to the world. They repeat the same message repeatedly in numerous ways. They use a variety of voices, media, and formats to share their vision and get you to buy what they are selling. It works!

You don't have millions. But what you do have is powerful. You, as a nonprofit organization with a clear vision for a better world, have:

- ✓ An important message
- ✓ That resonates with many
- ✓ And emotionally connects them to you.
- ✓ You have many voices to share your message and vision.

✓ Those voices include your employees, volunteers, board members, and donors.

Organizational growth counts on more and more people knowing and caring about your vision and your mission. Using your voice and inspiring everyone in your organization to use theirs creates an ever-growing nonprofit. It creates Sparkle!

Bring Sparkle! In-House

This (and more) is covered in the Sparkle! Action Plan, a private workshop for your organization. Go to www.nonprofitchampion.com/actionplan to learn more.

Does your organization Sparkle!?

Take The Nonprofit Champion Growth Readiness Assessment and find out. Go to www.nonprofitchampion.com/doyousparkle now.

Emotions Drive Decisions

Your donors, volunteers, and employees make decisions based on their emotions.

How about you?

Look in your closet. Chances are, you will spot an impulse purchase. That cute shirt that still has the tags on is proof of emotions driving decisions. Or you may make choices—from lottery tickets to vacation destinations—based on your "gut feeling." Again, emotions are the drivers.

You're not alone. In fact, researchers have discovered that decision-making is emotional, *and* without emotions, it is difficult to make choices. Even when you use data and logic, you may be using them to justify the decision you already made.

Making the Connection

You may see the value of an emotional connection with your prospective volunteers, donors, and advocates. When they feel moved by your vision, they relate to it and, as a result, are more likely to take action.

An emotional connection is what keeps them engaged, involved, and committed to your vision. That's just what your organization needs: more people who care.

What about all that data you've collected? Have it ready. Your prospects will call on logic from that other part of the brain to justify the decision to give and get involved. Facts and figures are there as backup, not the lead story.

Speaking of voices, I'd love to hear yours. Take a few minutes to share your vision with me at merle@non-profitchampion.com.

Your Path to Sparkle!

You started the journey with vision. Your big, sparkly vision is ready to share with the world. The way to do that is to use your voice and to inspire others to use theirs.

Your big takeaway from this section: You have a voice. Use it to make things happen.

Next, we will explore something fun and important: Stories. Learning to tell and use stories to grow your organization and raise more money is a key part of the Sparkle! process. Creating a Story Culture will move you forward on your journey to communicate better, raise more money, and grow faster.

Action Sheet – Voice

Every day, there are chances to speak about your vision.

What are some ways you might use your voice to share the vision of your organization?

How will you reach them?	Who will you reach?			
	Friends and family	Colleagues, funders, prospects	Chance meetings	Public
In-person				
Networking events				
Conversations				
Social media				
Newsletters				
Print media				
Email				
Grant applications				
Other				

Action Sheet – Voice

Discovering Opportunities to Share Your Vision

As you work to create a nonprofit full of people who are *happy, informed, willing, and able* to share their voices, you will see magic happen.

Your nonprofit will benefit when everyone is talking about the vision. To appeal to the broadest base, you need diverse voices. The more the message is shared, the more other people will know it, care about it, and act in a way that helps your organization grow.

Explore the possibilities to spread the word.

	Written	Spoken
One-on-one Conversations, emails, meetings	1. 2. 3. 4.	1. 2. 3. 4.
To a small audience Networking events, meetings, member-ship groups	1. 2. 3. 4.	1. 2. 3. 4.

To a crowd	1.	1.
Events, social media posts	2.	2.
	3.	3.
	4.	4.

STEP 3: STORY

Your Sparkle! Shines in Stories

You are ready for the journey to success. You have a clear vision and many voices to share it.

Now, you are ready to use those voices to bring your vision to life. One great way to do that is with the magic of stories. Storytelling is the proven way to reach an audience and inspire them to care, act, and give.

Read this section for a transformational secret formula that will empower your nonprofit.

Creating a Story Culture is central to the five steps to *Sparkle!* Get ready for opportunity and possibility as you learn how to use stories to grow your nonprofit organization.

It's like a fairytale come true.

Why a Story Culture?

Creating a Story Culture is at the core of Sparkle! This subtle yet powerful tool should come with a warning: may result in happier employees, donors, and board members.

Happiness is just the start. Stories are magical.

Making storytelling a part of your culture has many benefits:

- ✓ Stories make your workplace friendlier.
- ✓ Stories break down barriers, creating a more open, engaged staff and board.
- ✓ Stories inspire people to care about your organization and give time and money to support it.
- ✓ Stories are entertaining, and you deserve some fun!

From fairytales to sitcoms, stories are used to teach lessons, entertain, inspire action, inform, and motivate.

Stories are passed down through generations. Aesop shared his fables in the sixth century BC. Stories and parables in the Bible and Koran are known by millions around the world.

Every child knows the happy endings of *Sleeping Beauty* and the *Three Little Pigs*. And it would be hard to find an adult over 40 who doesn't know about Seinfeld's puffy shirt.

You, your family, and your organization have their own stories.

Stories are Sticky

Stories are often repeated. It's hard to memorize facts or lists, but stories stick. They are easily remembered and retold. When you hear a good story, chances are you will retell it.

Several years ago, I was running a fundraising event. One of the speakers was a young man, a father of three, who had formerly been homeless. I imagine that the 400 people in the room quickly forgot what the executive director said, what the meal was, or even that they attended. But I bet the dad's story stuck with them—not just the words but the feeling.

As Maya Angelou famously said, "I've learned that people will forget what you said, …but people will never forget how you made them feel."

Stories are Emotional

Decisions are driven by emotions. Stories evoke feelings. That's why stories are so important to your nonprofit success. Whether you tell it, share it in a post, or capture it in a video, a story is powerful.

Nonprofit organizations like yours may use stories to capture attention, share successes, and demonstrate the need for funds. Internally, they are a reward for hard work. Stories may motivate and inspire you to keep on going, even on tough days.

Want to add Sparkle! to your nonprofit consulting practice?

If you have experience working with nonprofit organizations and want to help your clients clarify their vision and use the Sparkle! Action Plan to raise more money and grow faster, take the first step to become a Certified Sparkle! Guide. Apply today at www.nonprofitchampion.com/certification.

Why A Story Culture

> *"A vibrant storytelling culture means the difference between whether your organization has a living, breathing portfolio of different stories, from different perspectives, that share its impact—or just a single, somewhat stagnant story."*
>
> —Stanford Innovation Social Review (SSIR)

Storytelling is a strategic, purposeful tool for non-profits. Stories have the power to engage, create awareness, drive change, and spark action.

A Story Culture adds Sparkle! to your organization. *It means having many stories from different perspectives to draw on whenever you want to share your message.* Stories are your go-to tool for a presentation, social media post, employee orientation, and fundraising ask.

SSIR goes on to say: "It's the difference between having one person in the organization dedicated to storytelling (whether that's the CEO, development director, or head of communications) and everyone in the organization having compelling stories at their fingertips."

With a Story Culture, *stories are valued and encouraged.* Your organization becomes a nurturing place where many voices are heard. An organization with a Story Culture believes that *everyone is a storyteller and every story is worth sharing.*

Your organization has stories to tell.

You have stories to tell.

How to Tell a Story

Becoming a good storyteller is a great life skill. Whether at work or play, your ability to tell stories will be an asset.

There are big, fat books written about how to tell a story. I'm going to share an easy formula. It is simple to remember because you've heard it many times before.

Here goes:

> *Once upon a time...*
>
> *Unfortunately...*
>
> *Thankfully...*
>
> *Happily ever after.*

That's it! This fairytale formula works like magic.

This secret to storytelling covers all the important points of a story. First, you have the set-up: how things were before something went wrong. Then, along comes the hero—that could be you or your organization—who, thankfully, saved the day.

The story arc is what adds drama and makes the story memorable.

This fairytale formula is easy to use to tell your personal stories and your organization's stories. You may soon find you are more entertaining and inspiring.

Practice telling your stories. It will quickly become natural.

Bring Sparkle! In-House

This (and more) is covered in the Sparkle! Action Plan, a private workshop for your organization. Go to www.nonprofitchampion.com/actionplan to learn more.

Does your organization Sparkle!?

Take The Nonprofit Champion Growth Readiness Assessment and find out. Go to www.nonprofitchampion.com/doyousparkle now.

Stories and Your Organization

Your organization has many stories to tell.

Earlier in this book, I shared my story about Juliette Low. The founder of Girl Scouts had a great impact on me as a seven-year-old Brownie. Since then, she has served as my inspiration and role model.

Founder Stories are Powerful

Most nonprofits, whether they are just starting out or 100 years old, have a person or small group of people who created the organization. A founder's story starts with a dream for a better world. It is a fairytale; it tells of a person seeing a need (unfortunately) and doing something about it (thankfully). The result is your organization.

Your founder's story may be a great asset as you begin to collect and share stories.

A couple of years ago, I was writing a keynote speech for a United Way CEO. I looked at the "About" page of the United Way Worldwide website (a very important page for your org, too!) for inspiration and discovered a great founder's story. The opening line is:

A Woman, a Priest, Two Ministers, and a Rabbi...

Imagine how easy my speech writing project was after that discovery. Chances are your founder story is a great opening line, also.

Successes, Big and Small

Your organization may capture the big stories, including anniversaries, large gifts, and new hires or board members. These help tell your story. But you may be missing some small yet powerful stories about your work.

You and others in your organization are doing important, meaningful work every day. You may make a big difference in someone's life.

Wow! That's worth sharing.

I call these little stories *Minor Miracles*. You are a miracle worker to those who count on you and your organization.

Sharing Minor Miracles is a great way to use your voice and encourage others to use theirs. Internally or externally, Minor Miracles tell a story that is uplifting, engaging, and rewarding.

Many Voices

Organizations hoping to communicate better, raise more money, and grow faster may use stories as a tool to reach those goals.

Creating a storytelling culture will:

- ✓ Increase your exposure to a broader audience
- ✓ Honor everyone in your organization as a valuable part of the culture
- ✓ Prepare you for opportunities and even create opportunities.

Sharing a vision and giving everyone a voice are key steps in building a Sparkle! organization. Using those voices to share stories increases the impact and results.

Collecting and Sharing Stories

On your journey to create a better world, you are building a strong, vibrant organization. There are many pieces that fit together to make that happen. Maybe the most important is building an ever-growing community of support. That requires resources.

Luckily, there are stories.

Strategic and purpose-driven storytelling is a resource for you to use to create awareness, engage communities, spark action, and drive change.

Stories help you raise money, attract volunteers, educate the board, develop partnerships, honor clients, and more.

Stories make it possible to package your work and share it with the world.

First, Make Room

When you see the value of stories, you may be inspired to clear space to make them part of your internal culture.

Start where you are. Consider which of these may work for you as you begin to use stories to communicate better, raise more money, and grow faster:

- Asking someone in your organization to be the keeper of stories
- Presenting a storytelling workshop using the fairytale formula
- Offering opportunities to share Minor Miracles
- Making storytelling a part of your regular meetings
- Asking clients to share their stories
- Encouraging board members and staff to discover their story with the *Why Me?* exercise from the previous section.

Your next team meeting might cover the value of stories, how to tell a story, or be an opportunity to share a Minor Miracle.

Have fun with stories. Celebrate success!

Next, Give Stories a Place

Stories are all around you. As a nonprofit, you are doing good work and creating stories the world wants to hear. Turning your work into memorable stories will give you a library of resources for fundraising and recruitment of staff, volunteers, board members, and clients.

The challenge—and opportunity—is to capture them so they are accessible and ready for sharing.

Like a database for donations, creating a way to file and retrieve stories gives you the tools you need for promotion, grants, and events. This can be as high-tech or low-tech as you need, depending on the size and budget of your organization.

To inspire and encourage the gathering of stories:

- ✓ Provide easy formats for creation.
- ✓ Offer accessible places to deposit them.
- ✓ Make it easy to retrieve and share stories.

You can capture Minor Miracles, your founder's story, and other important moments in many formats. An employee with a phone can create a video, or if the budget allows, you can hire a videographer to capture stories.

Your stories may be in words and pictures on paper, in computer files, or in video or audio format. Together, they create a full library of treasures ready for sharing.

One large research nonprofit asks everyone in the organization to share a Minor Miracle every month. These are often stories that would have been overlooked otherwise.

The employee sharing the story feels honored and valued.

Each month, one or more stories are written, recorded, or filmed to become part of the library. These little victories add up to a happy, healthy organization focused on success.

Finally, Spread Them Out

Sharing stories is a great way to get more of what you need. Every time you share a story, you have the opportunity to start a new relationship. Imagine where they may lead!

Which of these may work for you and your organization now or in the weeks ahead:

- Posting on social media (BONUS! Social sharing gives you a way to measure impact.)
- Seeking speaking opportunities in your community

- Providing story-sharing time at your next team meeting
- Showing a client testimonial video at your next event
- Sharing a story with local media, including newspaper or television
- Being a podcast guest to share success stories

Your Path to Fast Growth

With your Story Culture embedded in your organization, you are ready to continue your journey to Sparkle! You've used this leadership book to take you from vision to voice and now on to Synergy.

Bring Sparkle! In-House

This (and more) is covered in the Sparkle! Action Plan, a private workshop for your organization. Go to www.nonprofitchampion.com/actionplan to learn more.

Does your organization Sparkle!?

Take The Nonprofit Champion Growth Readiness Assessment and find out. Go to www.nonprofitchampion.com/doyousparkle now.

Once upon a time…

There was a mental health organization that celebrated its 50th anniversary. Theirs was a true success story. They had continually grown over the decades and were serving more people than ever.

Unfortunately…

The mental health counselors didn't feel appreciated. They loved the work, but burnout was a popular topic whenever they came up for air. Turnover was high.

Thankfully…

Several employees attended a nonprofit conference where the speaker talked about creating a happier, more sustainable organization—one with Sparkle!

When they heard about the benefits of giving employees the opportunity to share Minor Miracles, they were curious. Would this work for them?

They enthusiastically returned to work and tried it out. Yes, it is magical. The hard-working counselors have stories to share. Everyone feels inspired and motivated.

The bonus is a steady supply of success stories to share with donors!

Happily ever after…

Action Sheet – Story

Use this simple template to tell a story about a recent success you've had in your work or personal life.

Once upon a time…

Unfortunately…

Thankfully…

Happily ever after.

STEP 4: SYNERGY

Your Connections Create Sparkle!

Your path to more donors, larger gifts, engaged board members, active volunteers, and better service delivery starts with vision. With a clear, expressed vision for a better world, you begin the journey to communicate better, raise more money, and grow faster.

Your voice, combined with many diverse voices sharing dreams and stories, creates magic.

Now, it's time to explore how to use your newfound power to build a large network of people who care about your work. These are the folks who will donate, partner, and spread the word.

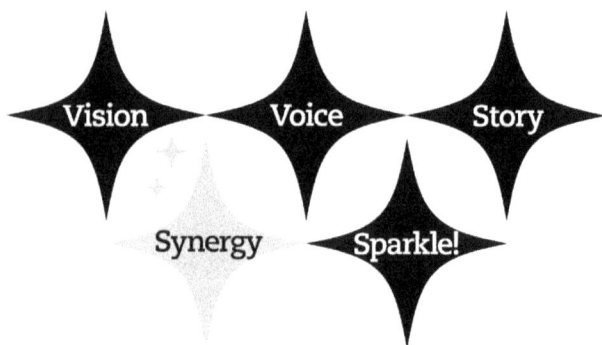

Vision Voice Story

Synergy Sparkle!

As a connected organization, new doors open for you. Synergy is a magical power.

You are ready for the next step: a clear path forward to build a bigger, better organization.

The possibilities are endless.

Synergy: Creating an Ever-Growing, Active Network

When everyone in your organization is *willing, able, and motivated* to share the vision, you have a non-profit organization with Sparkle!

But there's more.

Fast growth is dependent on a growing network of people—outside of your organization—who care about your work and support your nonprofit.

That support may come in the form of:

- ✓ Donations
- ✓ Partnerships
- ✓ Sponsorships
- ✓ Funding
- ✓ Joint projects
- ✓ Volunteer hours

You can build a fast-growth organization no matter what size you are now.

Synergy: Better Together

Synergy is about making connections. But it's more than that. Synergy is connecting with intention and shared goals.

You can find synergy in small and large ways. You may find it when you and others in your organization collaborate to reach a goal. You may find it when you partner with another organization that shares your vision (but has a different mission). And you may find it with a corporation or government agency supporting your work.

The way to grow a synergistic organization is to continually make connections. More connections equal more opportunities.

When you reach out to make connections and build your network, you may find:

- ✓ Natural synergy with those who are working toward the same vision
- ✓ Inspired synergy with those who care about your vision

Connecting to others who share your vision gives you natural partners. If you can identify a goal together, you can each do your part (your mission) to get you there. Instead of competition, you have synergy. Funders love it, and it is no wonder because it is efficient.

You and everyone in your organization can inform and inspire others. When you are actively making connections, you are on a fast track to growth.

Habitat for Humanity, a fast-growth organization, was founded in the 1970s. With a big dream
of building homes for families, they needed volunteers. They partnered with churches. These
well-established community institutions were able
to recruit volunteers to provide the needed labor.
That's synergy.

Use your imagination. Look beyond your immediate
circle. Who else has a stake in the game? Habitat
and the religious institutions they partner with share
a desire to do good work in the community and help
those in need.

Use this Action Sheet to explore. Imagine having
active relationships in your community in all sectors.
What might be possible?

Power in Numbers

You may feel like there are never enough hours in
the day.

It's not just you. Nonprofit leaders at every level tell
me they feel overworked. Even those who love their
work *and* are self-directed feel there isn't enough
time. You're trying to make the world a better place;
that's hard. To do that without adequate resources is
stressful.

You can't do it alone.

A lack of resources often means there is no quick fix for the problem. But there is a clear path forward.

Inspiring more and more people to learn about, care about, and do something about your nonprofit's work will make a difference.

With more people, all the good things you need are multiplied, and you may:

- ✓ Have more active volunteers
- ✓ Build a stronger board
- ✓ Increase donations from individuals, foundations, corporations, or the government
- ✓ Reach more of your ideal clients
- ✓ Expand your services and offerings
- ✓ Finally solve the one big problem you are facing now

Continually Making Connections

You may find that you—regardless of your position, seniority, or previous experience—can use your passion for the vision to be a connector. Start right where you are. Your message, desire, and enthusiasm will propel you forward.

Every Voice is a Connector

When your organization sparkles, everyone is *willing, able, and motivated* to use their voice to share the vision. That makes everyone a connector.

June Holley, a renowned pioneer in building community networks for social change, shared this story with me:

> I remember doing a network map for a hospital in Billings, Montana. There was a yellow dot on the map that represented somebody; all kinds of arrows were going into this person, and there were arrows going up. This person was extremely well-connected and important in the network. Yet none of the traditional leaders knew who this person was, even when they saw her name. This young, well-connected person had only been there for a year, but that whole time, she was playing a network-weaver role, actively connecting people and helping them get together and solve problems in the hospital.

"Yellow dot" was an active connector.

When everyone has a voice and uses it to connect, you create a networked organization. You have synergy. Your organization is in growth mode.

Being a Connector

Every connection holds possibility. Being a good connector will open doors for you and your nonprofit.

One way to get started is to make connections for others. This generous spirit helps those you meet. It also helps you as you build your network.

> I had a regular breakfast meeting with Kanani. I would walk into town to the diner, and there, we would share ideas, update each other on our work, and dish the dirt.
>
> One morning, I realized that every time I met Kanani, I came away with a list of connections. So right there, as I walked home, I decided that from then on, I would give Kanani as many connections as she gave me.
>
> And I did it!
>
> Being intentional, making a commitment to myself, and keeping it top of mind made me a great connector, too.

When I intentionally began making connections, it became part of the way I work. This practice made it possible for me to move to a new city and quickly become an active part of two communities: entrepreneurial start-ups and nonprofits.

How do you get started?

- ✓ Practice active listening. You want to know enough about the people you meet to put them in your mental database for future introductions.
- ✓ Get basic contact information from your new connections.
- ✓ Follow up. Send a quick message.
- ✓ Challenge yourself to make introductions.
- ✓ Use in-person introductions, email, and social media to increase connections and be a connector.

Imagine What Synergy Can Do for You

What if you could continually grow your network—not just adding names to a list but building an interconnected web of caring and support?

What if you had a steady flow of new people, finding synergy and aligning with your goals?

What if you felt that synergy every day?

Want to add Sparkle! to your nonprofit consulting practice?

If you have experience working with nonprofit organizations and want to help your clients clarify their vision and use the Sparkle! Action Plan to raise more money and grow faster, take the first step to become a Certified Sparkle! Guide. Apply today at www.nonprofitchampion.com/certification.

Once upon a time…

Kailin got her dream job. As a fundraiser, she was finally able to raise money for her favorite cause: stray animals.

Unfortunately…

Right from the start, Kailin could see problems. She had access to data but not to people. There was very little opportunity to interact with other staff members and volunteers. Plus, she was told it was too soon to talk to donors.

She wanted to hear more. She wanted the good news and to share it with donors and potential donors.

Thankfully…

Kailin overheard her coworkers talking about some changes happening in the organization. Soon, she was scheduled to attend a workshop.

Wow! Kailin was excited. In the training, everyone was encouraged to share stories and to make sharing a part of their nonprofit's culture. She could easily imagine how this new, upbeat environment would help her in her fundraising efforts.

Kailin quickly went from frustrated to excited about her job.

Happily ever after…

Synergy – Internal Sparks and External Sparks

Now, let's take a closer look at how Synergy works inside your organization. Then, I'll share some benefits you may experience outside of your organization as you interact with individuals, funders, and the public.

Internal Sparks: How Synergy Creates a Healthy Workplace

Synergy makes an organization hum. It's that special combination of sharing a vision, being *willing, able, and motivated* to contribute your voice, and prioritizing connection.

Synergy creates more of what you need to raise more money, deliver better service, and serve more people.

A synergistic workplace:

- ✓ Nurtures healthy working relationships
- ✓ Drives collaboration
- ✓ Promotes knowledge sharing
- ✓ Increases efficiency
- ✓ Makes you happy to be doing the good work

A vibrant, healthy organization is a growing one.

What you may have now	*What you could have*
Frustration	*Satisfaction*
Miscommunication	*Open dialogue*
Competition	*Teamwork*
Lack of information	*Access to information*

What's in it for You?

A synergistic organization is a great place to work. When you and those around you value making connections, you are a team.

Like a sports team working together toward a goal, each player/worker feels supported and motivated. When others have your back, it's a safe environment for creativity, experimentation, and exploration.

What's in it for Your Nonprofit?

A happy, healthy workplace is fertile ground for productivity. When there is a shared vision and a mindset to match, your organization is ready to connect with donors, partners, sponsors, and clients.

This spirit of belonging extends to volunteers and board members, giving them motivation and gratification.

These efforts to connect start inside your organization. Working toward synergy, your organization may:

- ✓ Leave space and time for networking
- ✓ Become a supportive environment where you feel more connected and aligned
- ✓ Inspire board members to use their connections
- ✓ Create a stronger, more creative, and sustainable nonprofit

Synergy is a feeling, a way of working, and a path to progress. Creating that synergy starts with connecting inside your organization.

Bring Sparkle! In-House

This (and more) is covered in the Sparkle! Action Plan, a private workshop for your organization. Go to www.nonprofitchampion.com/actionplan to learn more.

Does your organization Sparkle!?

Take The Nonprofit Champion Growth Readiness Assessment and find out. Go to www.nonprofitchampion.com/doyousparkle now.

External Sparks: How Synergy Drives Growth

Synergy is a result of openly engaging with others outside of your organization. Openly engaging with those who share your vision leads to opportunities.

You are doing important work. Rather than see others as competitors, see them as potential allies, ready to join you as you move toward your goals.

Through active networking, collaborating, brainstorming, and sharing, you may:

- ✓ Identify new opportunities
- ✓ Partner for greater impact
- ✓ Open new sources of funding
- ✓ Serve more clients
- ✓ Reach a broader audience
- ✓ Attract larger donations

Your journey to build a stronger nonprofit, raise more money, and grow faster starts when you ask, "What can we do better together?"

Start with an Open Mind

Your synergy with another nonprofit, government agency, or local business may be as simple as sharing ideas or offering connections. It may be as complex as partnering on a program or creating a joint entity.

Be open to possibilities.

Think about Habitat for Humanity and its relationship with churches. Start by identifying which organizations share your vision. Then, explore how you may make a connection.

There are excellent free tools available, including Liberating Structures, an app with a variety of interaction methods for exploring and collaborating. Network Weaver offers a full library of free and low-cost tools for building networks.

Start Where You Are

Synergy happens when people work together to make something big happen.

You may be part of the growth and success wherever you are in the organization.

You may think of yourself as a leader, no matter where you are in the organization. Effective leadership may be redefined as *practicing critical and collaborative thinking and taking action where you are right now.*

Be a Sparkler!

This new approach to leadership offers everyone the chance to grow and develop their skills while building a network of support for the nonprofit.

A Sparkler:

1. Actively engages with others inside and outside the organization
2. Practices and promotes teamwork
3. Advances the vision by sharing it with others
4. Keeps learning
5. Cares about others' success
6. Takes action in response to what is in front of them

Don't wait for a promotion. Look around and see where your critical thinking may make a difference. Reach out to connect and collaborate.

At every level, there is the opportunity to be a team player, build a network, and inspire others. When you and everyone in your nonprofit are connecting, you are moving in the right direction.

Are you already in a management role? When you empower employees, volunteers, and board members by giving them the tools, resources, and confidence to speak and connect, they contribute to building a diverse, sustainable community of support for your organization.

Action Sheet – Synergy

Your Synergy Network

Take a few minutes to reflect on your connections. List two or three key associates or groups in each category.

Foundations

_____
_____
_____

Individuals

_____
_____
_____

Corporations

_____
_____
_____

Government

_____
_____
_____

Small Businesses

_____
_____
_____

Action Sheet – Synergy

Business Type	Organization	Person	Connections
Nonprofit			
Foundation			
Small Business			
Corporate			
Government			

Create your dream list of connections. Begin by naming organizations that may share your visions. List a person in each organization who may be a good contact for you. Finally, explore the connections you may already have with each person and organizations.

Have fun with it: put each name on a sticky note and build your network map on the wall. See who else in your organization has connections with those you identified.

STEP 5: SPARKLE!

Your Time to Sparkle!

You started the journey with Vision. Your big, sparkly Vision is ready to share with the world. The way to do that is to use your voice and to inspire others to use theirs. You discovered the secret of story and the role it plays in a vibrant, healthy nonprofit. Plus, you are creating a joyful place to work where you and your coworkers are moving forward together in synergy.

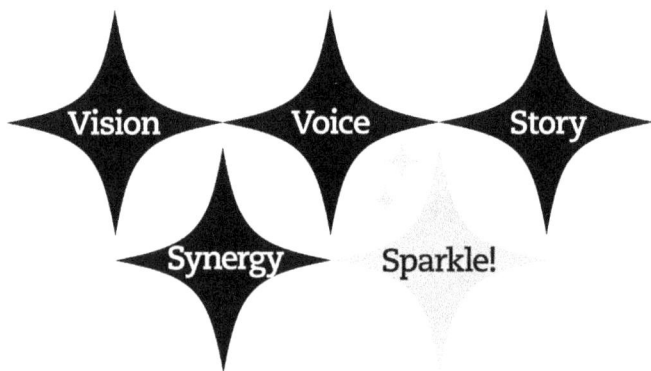

Your big takeaway from this section: You are a Sparkler! ready to build and make your dreams come true.

In the final section of this book for nonprofits, you will find practical ways to add Sparkle! as you work to build an organization that communicates better, raises more money, and grows faster.

Sparkle! Creating Your Best Organization

You and your organization deserve to shine.

Visionary nonprofits like yours grow and prosper. Dreams do come true.

You have the tools to communicate better, raise more money, and grow faster. This book has taken you on a path from vision to Voice to Story to Synergy. These are key elements you need for ongoing, continual success.

Loving Where You Are

What does it look like when a nonprofit Sparkles!?

- ✓ It's a *happy place* to be. You look forward to going to work.
- ✓ There's a feeling that we are *better together*.
- ✓ Everyone sees and works toward a *clear direction* for the future.
- ✓ Each person *feels heard* and *appreciates the diversity* of voices.
- ✓ *Growth, opportunity, and aspirations* are valued.

✓ The energy is *fully aligned*. You feel you are contributing to a bigger goal and that together, you can achieve more.

Sparkle! is for you, no matter where you are in your organization. Each volunteer, employee, and board member deserves to feel that their work is personally fulfilling and serves a purpose. You are part of a great cause.

Sparkle! Every Day

Let's explore some ideas for using Sparkle! in your nonprofit. You may think of it as a fresh approach to solving problems, a way to introduce ideas, or a whole new way to work.

Meetings

They say everyone hates meetings, but that's not what nonprofit employees tell me. One of the big complaints I hear is there are not enough meetings. Employees want to be informed, they want to share ideas, and they want teamwork. A good meeting meets these needs and inspires action.

How to add Sparkle! to your organization with meetings:

Vision: Keeping vision front and center is a reminder of your purpose and gives everyone a clear goal. Go for the feeling of "we are in this together."

Voice: Giving everyone a chance to be heard. Frustration comes from not having the chance to speak or having the same person(s) speak repeatedly.

Story: Stories get everyone paying attention. Use your regular meetings as a time to share Minor Miracles or other stories.

Synergy: Connection starts internally. Provide time and space for everyone in the meeting to network and find common ground.

Regularly scheduled meetings are something to look forward to when everyone participates.

Diversity, Equity, and Inclusion

Nonprofits may understand the value of inclusion, but many struggle to make it part of the culture. Building a diverse organization is not done in an annual workshop or with written policies. It is an ongoing practice.

How Sparkle! encourages DE&I:

Vision: Weaving the practice of sharing dreams and goals into your work brings people together, giving them common ground.

Voice: With a shared understanding and goal and everyone in your organization *willing, able, and motivated* to use their voice, you are moving toward equity.

Story: Keeping a Story Culture alive creates a full, diverse, rich trove of stories that are honored and shared.

Synergy: Connecting with an ever-expanding circle, with diversity as a core value, is celebrated and appreciated.

With Sparkle! diversity, equity, and inclusion are woven into your organization, actively contributing to its growth and success.

Strategic Game Plan

Sparkle! turns what you may find as an arduous task into a journey for discovery, growth, and reward. With planning, sharing, and checking as part of your regular practice, you are always strategic, and big gains are within reach.

How Sparkle! reimagines strategic planning:

Vision: Focusing on dreams and goals year-round makes planning an easier, more efficient process, one you may actually look forward to doing.

Voice: Employees, service recipients, and board members are all heard, giving you a realistic view of the past and fresh ideas for the future.

Story: Telling stories allows you to share your plans in a form that engages and motivates.

Synergy: A connected organization makes plans that work for everyone while emphasizing the importance of growth through synergy.

No more complaining about plans collecting dust or not enough voices being heard, your Sparkle! Game Plan is a living map to a big, better future.

Evaluation and Measurement

Measuring outcomes—the results of your work—helps you continually improve. It may be a requirement of a grant maker or government partner or simply a desire to do your best. By creating objectives, gathering feedback, and collecting and sharing data, you will meet standards and, hopefully, go above and beyond to provide excellent service.

How Sparkle! helps you measure your success:

Vision: Your clear vision and mission clarify your objectives, helping you decide what to measure and why.

Voice: With continual feedback from all constituents, data collection and sharing is easy and ongoing.

Story: Using stories to gather, collect, and share your work and experiences brings results to life.

Synergy: A synergistic network where sharing is expected and celebrated makes community-wide measurement a real possibility.

Go above and beyond with Sparkle! all year long.

Fundraising

Every nonprofit faces the challenge of raising more money. Whether it is from individual donations, grants, sponsorships, or earned income, seeking funds is time-consuming. Often, organizations invest precious time and resources in fundraising that does little to advance the vision and mission of the organization.

How Sparkle! improves fundraising results:

Vision: With a focus on vision, you are creating an inspired and appealing message that can be used in asks, grants, and media.

Voice: Greater exposure and opportunity are the result of many voices sharing your vision, resulting in a larger base of support, the discovery of funding sources, and motivated employees and volunteers.

Story: Placing stories at the center of your fund-raising events and appeals generates increased caring, support, and giving.

Synergy: Asking for money is easier and more successful when you have an ever-growing network that knows and shares your vision. Plus, partnerships are attractive to funders, resulting in more grants and larger gifts.

Sparkle! creates a momentum that builds over time. The result is more money, more opportunity, and faster growth.

Hiring, Onboarding, and Retention

Employee turnover is expensive. Managers tell me they can't keep employees, while employees tell me they are unhappy with the lack of opportunity. Creating a workplace that offers opportunity and gratification may make a difference for your organization.

How Sparkle! results in happy employees:

Vision: Engaging employees in the vision from the start creates a group connected by a common purpose. Connecting and engaging employees and volunteers results in motivated workers.

Voice: Focusing on enabling every person to be *willing, able, and motivated* to share the vision means everyone feels respected and honored.

Story: Hearing, sharing, and repeating stories creates a strong sense of belonging and community.

Synergy: As a result of empowering your employees with a key role as a connector, everyone is, and feels, important.

Creating a welcoming environment and offering a commitment to communication and connection means employees are engaged and likely to stay.

Service Delivery

When your goal is to do your best work for the most people, you may need to remove obstacles, optimize the work environment, and get all the support you can find. It's a never-ending challenge for many nonprofit organizations as the demand for service continues to increase.

Vision: With a focus on vision, you know who else serves the same people, so optimizing service delivery and effectiveness may become easier.

Voice: Respected employees and volunteers often feel motivated to work smarter and harder, potentially optimizing service.

Story: Hearing stories from those who benefit from your organization inspires you and others, potentially improving outcomes for those you serve.

Synergy: Your ever-growing network increases opportunities for partnering to provide more and better service and outcomes. Plus, this enables you to get more clients through connections.

Sparkle! gives you the power to communicate better, provide better service, and grow faster.

See a gold Sparkler? That means this (and more) is covered in the Sparkle! Action Plan, a private workshop for your organization. Go to www.nonprofitchampion.com/actionplan to learn more.

Put Some Sparkle! in Your Future

You deserve some Sparkle! You've earned it.

Your work is so important. You shouldn't have to waste energy on poor communication, misinformation, struggles for funding, or any other obstacles holding you back.

It's time to take a fresh approach.

That's what Sparkle! is.

It's a way to live and work every day that offers hope and opportunity—the very things that created your nonprofit organization.

Sparkle! is designed to fit into your everyday life. There's no need to invest or refocus. It's more of an attitude, a frame of mind. Sparkle! makes your organization a place to dream, share, and deliver.

Every nonprofit, including yours, has the potential to communicate better, raise more money, and grow faster. That's Sparkle!

WRAPPING IT UP

If, like me, you read the last page first, welcome to this book. It is all about creating happy, healthy non-profit organizations that will make the world a better place.

Throughout these pages, I've shared what I know from experience, what I've learned from research, and what I've seen others do successfully.

I've also seen lots of mistakes. I've talked to hundreds of unhappy nonprofit employees, and I was once one myself. The work you do is too important to waste time because of poor communication, lack of direction, and unclear goals.

I hope this book inspires you to continue to do the good work. Whatever the size or purpose of your organization, it may need some Sparkle!

Sparkle! is the magic that happens when you start with a clear vision and are willing, able, and motivated to use your voice. Sharing stories deepens connections and inspires caring. Those connections become donors, clients, sponsors, and partners. And the cycle continues.

You can make magic.

Spread the word. Encourage everyone in your organization to read this book; share your copy today. When you are ready for more, contact me to schedule a workshop.

I'm cheering you on. I believe in you.

Make your own Sparkle!

Share your stories with me. I'd love to hear how you have added Sparkle! to your organization.

Visit Nonprofitchampion.com/Sparkle and reach me directly at merle@nonprofitchampion.com.

I'm also on LinkedIn at linkedin.com/in/merlebenny.

Ready for More?

Work Directly with Merle and Take a Big Leap Forward

Want to add Sparkle! to your nonprofit consulting practice?

If you have experience working with non-profit organizations and want to help your clients clarify their vision and use the Sparkle! Action Plan to raise more money and grow faster, take the first step to become a Certified Sparkle! Guide. Apply today at www.nonprofitchampion.com/certification.

Want your team to work together to achieve more?

Walking your team through the Sparkle! Action Plan is your path to aligning your team, growing your nonprofit, and creating common goals and language that excites and inspires your team. You'll spend two days clarifying your message, honing your stories, and building connections while unifying your team. The private workshop at your location will transform your organization. More information at www.nonprofitchampion.com/training.

ACKNOWLEDGMENTS

Thank you, Nonprofit Champions. The world is a better place because of the work you do. I am humbled and inspired by your dedication.

This book is my way of passing on all I have learned from the great nonprofit founders and leaders I've had the opportunity to work with, including Agnes Land, Mary Robinson, Karen Olson, and Patrick Morrissy.

I am grateful to my mother. She was a successful nonprofit professional and my greatest inspiration. My sister Jeanne followed her example and became an outstanding executive director.

My father was a great storyteller, and my brother, Mark, has continued the tradition. I learned how stories have the power to captivate, influence, and move audiences from them.

My sister Jo-Anne has been keeping me on my toes since the day I was born. Her creativity and social skills are unmatched.

My business and life partner, Joe Landi, has inspired, supported, and improved my work from day one.

Thank you to Ben Gioia for your smile, guidance, and inspiration.

Thank you to the Association of Nonprofit Specialists in New York City, my professional community.

Finally, I acknowledge the Sparks in my life: my children, Joy, John, and Sarah. XO